Comic Capers

Written and illustrated by
Laura Ellen Anderson and Robin Boyden

Contents

Super-Duper Cat

4

6

9

15

CALLING ALL SECRET AGENTS!
Do you have what it takes to be a member of the FLEA.I.A?
Prove your secret agent abilities by completing the tasks below!

TASK ONE:
A couple of sneaky foxes escaped our grasp and have stolen Mrs Pawprints' food!

The foxes have caused quite a mess, so you'll need to look carefully. We've given you a list of the food you need to find!

Burger	Cake	Apple	Sandwiches	Baked beans
Pineapple	Egg		Bananas	Grapes
Fish	Chicken drumsticks	Pizza	Doughnut	Chips

Did you find all of the food ...? GOOD JOB!
To prove you're a TRUE secret agent, you must complete one more task!

TASK TWO:
Get a piece of paper to write on. Next, crack the code on the right to reveal your very own TOP SECRET FLEA.I.A password! Once you've cracked the code, keep your password in a safe place.

L J Q W F R W K O
L K Q D B X X

| A | B | C | D | E | F | G | H | I | J | K | L | M | N | O | P | Q | R | S | T | U | V | W | X | Y | Z |
| Z | A | Y | B | X | C | W | D | V | E | U | F | T | G | S | H | R | I | Q | J | P | K | O | L | N | M |

Need a hand? The **RED** letters correspond to the **BLACK** letters.
Example: **D** = **B** and **J** = **E**

Now you're an OFFICIAL FLEA.I.A member, you can use the code
to write your own secret notes with your friends!

Ralph, Riko and Pickle Seek Bigfoot

Something's not right at Riko's house, and it has nothing to do with Pickle the dog's missing dinner.

When's dinner?

But I'm hungry!

DO NOT DISTURB

Woof!

Hmm ...

No, no, no. This won't do at all!

I'm never going to win the Wildfest World Photochamp competition with boring pet photos.

Oh dear. I'd better cheer him up.

In the 20 years I've been a pet photographer, not once have I even reached the first round of the competition.

The pets' little faces are so innocent, so cute, so lacking in exotic danger. Where is the drama in a hamster?

Argh! If I see one more cute animal in a costume I'll explode!

Sigh.

SOB!

Huh? Riko! What's the matter?

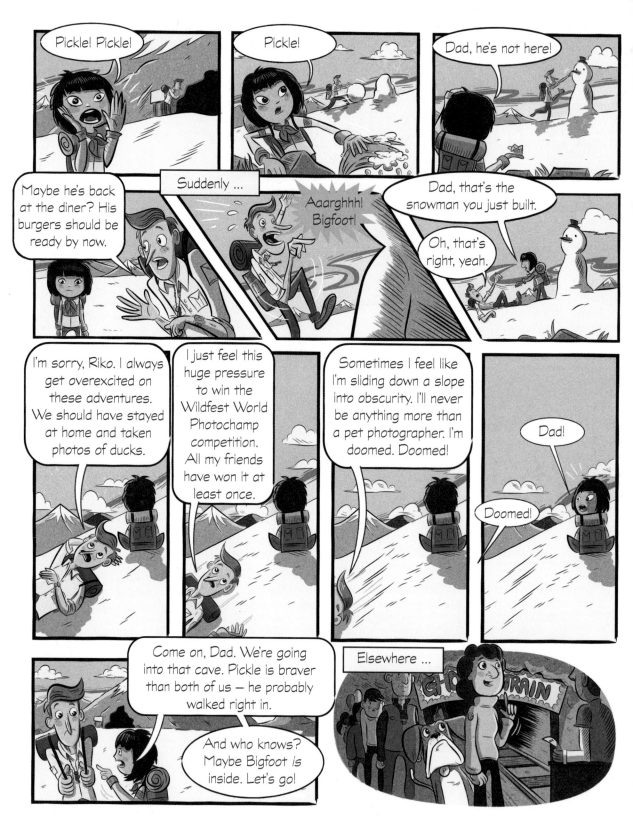

33

Ralph is about to take off on his next adventure. Can you help him to understand what each dial in his plane measures? Check your answers at the bottom of the page.

a) How confused Ralph is.
b) How high the plane is flying.
c) How tall the passengers are.

a) How long it will take to fly home.
b) How empty Ralph's stomach is.
c) How full the fuel tank is.

a) How fast the plane is travelling.
b) How hard the wind is blowing.
c) How far it is to the nearest doughnut shop.

ALTIMETER
HEIGHT / FEET

30
FUEL GAUGE
10
70
EMPTY   FULL

16
14   18
RPM
12   20
28   22
AIRSPEED
24

What do you get if you cross an ice cream with some land surrounded by water?
A dessert island!

What do you call a naughty girl who refuses to tidy up her clothes?
The Sock Mess Monster!

The Loch Ness Monster

Legend status   9
Fear Factor   5
Maximum Roar   7
Hiding Ability   8

Make your own monster game!

There are lots of amazing legendary creatures, so why don't you keep track of them all by making your own monster card game?

Draw your favourite monsters on pieces of card and give them scores out of ten in categories such as 'Fear Factor' or 'Maximum Roar'. Once you've made at least ten cards, challenge a friend to a game.

Rules: Divide the pack evenly between the players. One player picks a category from their first card and says what the score is for that category. The player with the highest score for that category wins the other player's card and chooses the next category. The winner is the first player to collect all the cards.

Example monsters: Griffin, Sabre Tooth Tiger, Medusa, Dragon, Kraken.

Answers: 1 b   2 c   3 a

Two hours later ...

I wish I could cheer Riko up.

Of course! Here's present number two!

A Nessie snow globe. I love it! Thanks, Dad.

Wait, are we here to look for another made-up monster?

Uh ... no! We're here to go canoeing and relax in the sun.

Hey look, here's our hotel. Wow, it's huge!

It's nice here, isn't it, Riko?

Hmm, yeah, it's OK.

Hi, I'm Pickle. What's your name?

I'm Rosie, and I guard the hotel. Grrr!

Snow! We can go and bury things in it!

I love digging in the snow, too.

LOCH NESS

LOCH NESS EXPRESS

39

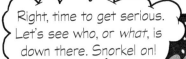 Right, time to get serious. Let's see who, or *what*, is down there. Snorkel on!

Wow, it's amazing down here. Look at all these treasures! But where is Nessie? I'd better dive a bit deeper ...

Up above, more snow fell and Loch Ness began to freeze ...

and freeze ...

and freeze.

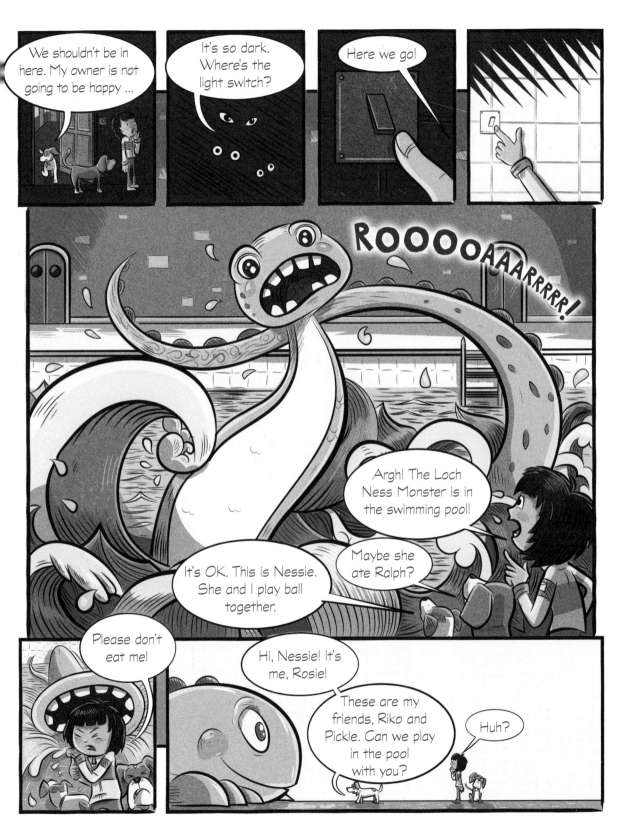

WHOOSH

All this fun is making me hungry!

Wheeee!

But how did Nessie get in your swimming pool?

STOP! You shouldn't be in here!

Along a river that runs under the hotel from Loch Ness itself. There were so many tourists trying to take photos of her, she was too scared to stay in the lake.

If people knew she really did exist then she'd be pestered more than ever. We're protecting her. Please don't tell a soul.

Nessie's secret is safe with me. Shhhh!

I'd tell Dad about Nessie if I thought he could keep a secret!

Wait, Dad's still missing. Where is he?

RIKO! QUICK!

What can you see out there, Pickle? Is it Dad?

Who would be daft enough to take a canoe out in a snow storm?

About the authors

Laura Ellen Anderson is a children's book illustrator and comic artist who was born holding a pencil and paper. When she's not drawing, Laura is probably pretending to be a superhero, or even better, Super-Duper Cat!

When Robin Boyden was younger he began to write and draw his own books because the library wouldn't let him borrow as many as he wanted. Robin enjoys putting his comic creations into ridiculous situations – which characters like Ralph, Riko and Pickle then have to get themselves out of!